By Jim Drewett

CONTENTS

INTRODUCTION

*R*ugby was invented in 1823 when a pupil at Rugby School in England picked up a football and ran with it. The game now holds pride of place as the national sport in ten countries. Rugby's forward-propelling, bulldozing pace combined with its sophisticated strategy has made it one of the world's best-loved sports.

To an outsider, rugby can seem confusing. But at its most basic, it's about running with an oval-shaped ball to score points. For this reason, anyone of any age, at any level, can enjoy the game. We hope this book will inspire you to get out there scoring tries.

CONTACT IN RUGBY

Rugby is a full-contact sport and players must show discipline and self-control at all times. Violent behaviour, such as kicking and punching, is not tolerated. The types of contact in the game are also different for different age groups (see the Rules section on pages 46–47). Make sure you are aware of what is allowed on the field, and what is not.

THE PITCH

Rugby is played with an oval ball on a grass pitch. The pitch is marked with straight chalk lines with H-shaped goalposts at either end. But you don't need a lot of equipment to play rugby. Once you have a pair of boots and a ball, you are ready to have a throw-around with your friends.

THE PITCH

The rugby pitch is made up of two parts – the field of play, and the in-goal areas. Most of the action happens in the field of play, which is 100 metres long and 70 metres wide. At either end of the pitch are the in-goal areas, which must be between 10 and 22 metres deep, and 70 metres wide. This is where players touch the ball down to score a try.

THE GOALPOSTS

The goalposts are H-shaped structures positioned at either end of the field of play, on the tryline. The two upright posts must be five to six metres apart, and they are joined by a crossbar three metres above the ground. The minimum height of the goalposts is 3.4 metres above the crossbar.

THE OFFICIALS

A rugby game is controlled by a single referee, who runs around on the pitch with the players. The referee is helped by two touch judges, who decide if a player has scored a try and whether the ball is out of play.

THE TEAMS

Each team has 15 players, divided into forwards and backs. There are eight forwards (wearing the numbers 1 to 8) and seven backs (numbered 9 to 15). These players have different roles on the rugby pitch – the forwards win the ball, and the backs score the points.

FLAGS

There are 14 flags on the rugby pitch to indicate where the boundaries are. Four of the flags are positioned at either end of the pitch to mark out the in-goal areas. The other six flags are outside the playing area, marking the touchlines, the 22-metre lines and the halfway lines.

DEAD-BALL LINE:
Once the ball goes over this line
it is 'dead', or out of play.

IN-GOAL AREA:
Where players touch down
the ball to score a try.

5-METRE LINE:
The players must stand
behind this line when
there is a line-out.

TOUCHLINE:
Once the ball goes
over these lines,
it is 'in touch' and
out of play.

10-METRE LINE:
When the game starts,
the ball must be kicked
over this line for the
kick to be legal.

**15-METRE
DASH LINE:**
Scrums and penalties
are taken on the
15-metre dash line
after line-out
infringements.

**HALFWAY
DASH LINE:**
Kickoffs and
restarts are taken
from here.

HALFWAY LINE:
Where the game
starts and is
restarted
after a try.

**5-METRE
DASH LINE:**
Marks the distance
from the defending
team's goal line
where a scrum,
line-out or penalty
can be taken.

**22-METRE
LINE:**
Drop-outs in
adult rugby
are taken
from this line.

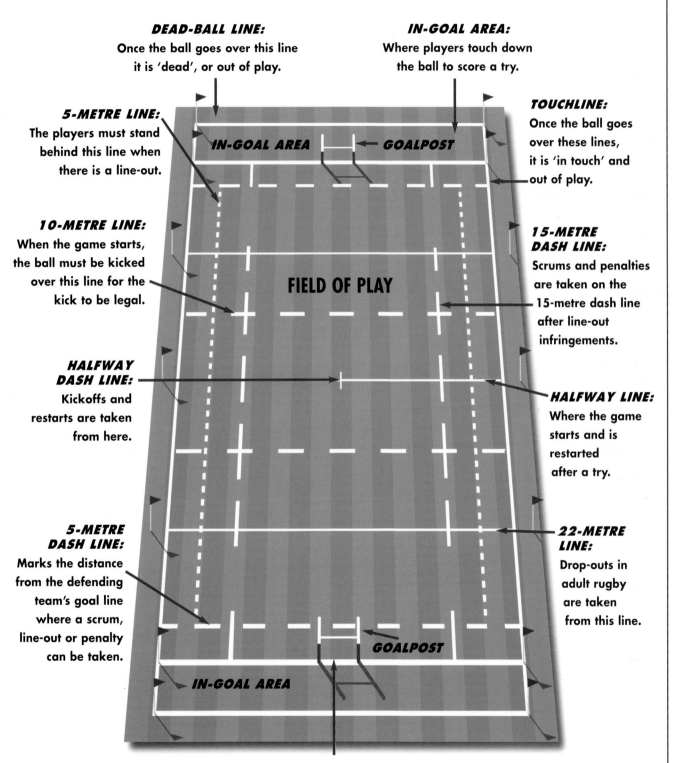

IN-GOAL AREA   GOALPOST

FIELD OF PLAY

GOALPOST

IN-GOAL AREA

TRYLINE:
Also called the goal line, players must
reach the tryline to score a try.

POSITIONS

*E*ach rugby player's position comes with its own requirements, skills and responsibilities. Young rugby players should try out every position at one time or another, to find the best fit. Regardless of position, every rugby player should be able to run, pass, catch and tackle.

FORWARDS

1 LOOSE HEAD PROP
A prop's major role is to support the hooker in scrums, as well as supporting in the line-out, rucks and mauls. The prop should also be as challenging to the opposition as possible when they have the ball.

2 HOOKER
The hooker is at the centre of the scrum and uses his feet to 'hook' the ball to the back of the scrum. Hookers normally throw the ball in at line-outs. The hooker's job is the most dangerous and requires great skill.

3 TIGHT HEAD PROP
The tight head prop has to keep the scrum locked and stop it going backwards. They need to take a lot of weight, so a tight head prop needs to be physically strong.

4 SECOND ROW (LOCK)
The role of the second row is to lock and push in the scrum. The locks have to be good jumpers and are primary targets at line-outs.

5 SECOND ROW (LOCK)
The role of the number 5 shirt is much the same as the number 4 — to win the ball. Both second row players need to be strong and fit.

6 BLINDSIDE FLANKER
The blindside flanker binds to the scrum on the side nearest to the touchline. Both flankers have the fewest set of responsibilities but are expected to provide forward movement of play and gain possession.

7 OPENSIDE FLANKER
The openside flanker binds to the side of the scrum furthest away from the touchline, and is the first to secure the loose ball and get it into play after a ruck or maul. The position requires a lot of running — so the player needs a very high level of fitness.

8 NUMBER 8
The number 8 co-ordinates scrums, rucks and mauls with the scrum half. In a scrum, the number 8 passes the hooker's ball to the scrum half or collects it from the back of a scrum to begin an attack. The number 8 can also be the line-out jumper or support.

BACKS

9 SCRUM HALF
The scrum half connects the backs with the forwards. The scrum half usually dictates the direction of play and is responsible for putting the ball into the scrum and often collecting it to begin the attack. The scrum half can also make the decisions in a line-out.

10 FLY HALF
The fly half is one of the most influential players on the pitch, responsible for most of the goal kicking: defensive and positional. As the leader of the back line, the fly half has to be a fast and evasive runner, able to react quickly to situations, both in attack and defence.

11 LEFT WING
The left wing suits players who are stronger on their left side: they step better off their left foot and pass better from their left hand. The winger also needs to have enough pace to get to the front of the pitch, and then run back to support the backs.

12 INSIDE CENTRE
The inside centre is like a bigger and heavier fly half. The number 12 can't be afraid to tackle and needs to be able to pass quickly under pressure. Kicking skills are also necessary as the centre is a natural place to send out the ball to either side of the pitch.

13 OUTSIDE CENTRE
The number 13 needs to be strong and fast, and keep the ball in a tackle. The role is a lot like that of the inside centre, but the player is not usually physically as big.

14 RIGHT WING
Both the right and left wingers need a lot of pace. But the right wing gets the ball more often than the left. The number 14 needs to able to run fast and have exceptional evasion skills.

15 FULLBACK
The fullback is the last line of defence. The number 15 needs to be able to tackle well and catch a high ball. The fullback also needs to collaborate with the wingers to get the ball up the field.

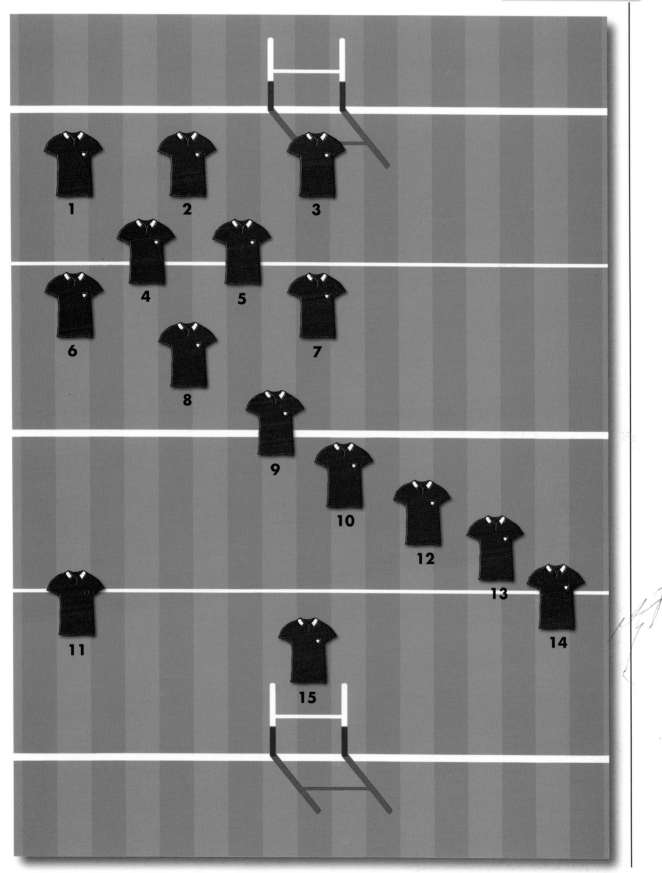

EQUIPMENT

Rugby is a full-contact sport. It is important to have the right equipment, for your own protection and for the safety of other players. No metal is allowed on the field, except the metal in boot studs. Even eyeglasses are forbidden.

THE BALL

Rugby union is played with an oval-shaped ball, traditionally made of leather but more recently from waterproof material.
- *All balls must be between 28–30cm in length (11–13 inches).*
- *Most adult balls weigh between 383–440g (13.5–15.5oz).*

HEAD PROTECTION

Many rugby players wear protective headgear to prevent head injuries and cuts. These can sometimes occur in rucks, mauls and scrums.
- *Headgear is used most often by forwards and is usually made from lightweight plastic material.*

UPPER BODY PROTECTION

Upper body protection stops injury around the chest and shoulders, which take a lot of impact during tackles.
- *Protection usually takes the form of strong, lightweight padding.*

SHORTS

Shorts are traditionally made from cotton.
- *They sometimes come with reinforced stitching to prevent tearing.*

In the past rugby shirts were made from cotton, but these days lightweight synthetic shirts are more common.

- *If you are buying a rugby shirt for training make sure you get the right fit. A shirt should not be too small or it could rip. If it is too big, your opponents can grab and hold you more easily.*

The gum shield, or mouth guard, protects your teeth, gums and jaw.

- *Everyone has a different-shaped mouth, so a gum shield needs to be properly moulded to fit.*
- *A dentist can fit a shield, or you can buy a self-moulding one from a sports shop.*

Traditionally, rugby boots were cut higher than football boots. Today, different players favour different types of boots:

- *Kickers like a well-fitting boot, similar to a footballer's.*
- *Forwards and props prefer a high ankle cut, to provide support in scrums.*
- *Leather and synthetic boots are available, as are boots that are made of both. Certain boots come with the option to change studs, depending on the pitch conditions.*
- *Knee-length socks with turnover tops are also worn.*

There are generally three types of boot: the six-stud, eight-stud or nine-stud.

- *The eight- or nine-stud boot is popular with props, hookers and locks to provide them with extra grip during scrums and mauls.*
- *The six-stud boot is favoured by the backs, who need a lighter boot for quick movement.*
- *Blades are a modern adaptation of studs, chosen for their lightweight grip.*
- *A longer stud is used for wet, muddier conditions and a shorter stud for dry.*

BALL FAMILIARISATION

Whether it's catching, passing or holding – controlling a rugby ball is what the game is about. It's important to spend time getting to know the shape and feel of the ball. These drills will help you. To familiarise yourself with the rugby pitch, practise on one as much as you can.

HANDLING DRILL

This drill can be performed alone or in a group. Make sure there is enough space between players.

Stand holding a rugby ball with your legs apart. Pass the ball five times: around the head, around the waist, around the knees, around the ankles, and between the legs in a figure of eight. Now throw the ball into the air, taking one step forward and catching it behind your back.

HANDLING RELAY

This drill is designed to help players practise passing between each other in areas of space. You will need one ball, five to nine players, and half a rugby pitch.

The aim is for players A and B to reach the tryline. Starting at the halfway line, players A and B run down the pitch towards the tryline. The ball is thrown between them, until either A or B scores.

The three defenders try to stop them. They stand in a line up the field about 10 metres apart. Initially the defenders mark A only. Once the players are more confident, both A and B can be marked.

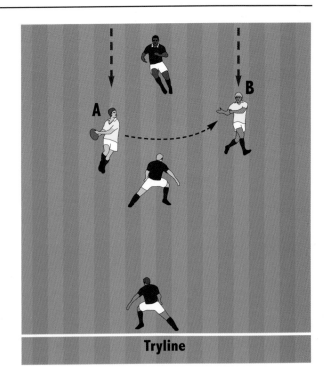

Tryline

THE NEED FOR SPEED

Being quick on your feet is an invaluable skill to have as a rugby player. The really good players can not only run fast, but can also change their pace. They can slow down and then speed up suddenly to avoid being tackled or to score a try. These drills will help you with your pace.

FAST FEET

You will need one or more players for this drill.

The players stand on the touchline facing the 5-metre line. They race to the 5-metre line — using as many steps as they can. The object is to complete as many tiny steps in the shortest amount of time possible.

BALL TAG

For this drill you will need four cones, a ball, and at least six players.

First create a square using the cones, about 10 metres apart. Choose three taggers, who have to tag the rest of the players – the evaders – with the ball. The evaders run from cone to cone. The taggers stand in the square and try to tag the evaders. Once tagged the evaders have to stand still. The taggers can pass the ball to each other, but once they have possession they can only move one foot.

TOP TIP
To surprise your opponents, combine a change of speed with a change of direction.

EVASION

In rugby, learning to evade opponents is essential. Variation of pace, swerving and side-stepping are all moves rugby players need to know — especially if they are backs or scrum halves.

THE DUMMY

The aim of the dummy is to fool your opponent into believing you are about to make a pass.

STEP 1

Run towards the defender while holding the ball.

STEP 2

Look towards a team-mate and swing your arms as if you are going to pass to him.

STEP 3

Don't release the ball to your team-mate. As the defender looks towards your team-mate, swerve and accelerate forward into the space you have just created.

THE SIDESTEP

The sidestep is a favourite among backs, as a way of losing defenders with quick footwork.

STEP 1

As you approach the defender, choose which side you are going to run past. Shorten your stride.

STEP 2

Now step wide and put your weight onto your outside leg as if you are about to move that way.

STEP 3

As the defender moves sideways to grab you, shift your body weight to the other leg and take off.

STEP 4

With the defender moving the wrong way, you can accelerate past him.

The swerve is another way of evading defenders. It is more subtle than the sidestep. It is popular with wingers.

STEP 1

Run straight towards the defender, holding the ball in both hands.

STEP 2

Start to slant your running line slightly away from the defender. Hold the ball on the opposite side to the defender and move to that side. On the edge of your feet, lean away from the defender in the direction you want to go.

STEP 3

Pick up pace and accelerate.

> Keep your eyes on the defender throughout this move.

STEP 1

As you run, watch the defender. Keep the ball on the opposite side to him.

STEP 2

When he attempts to tackle you, stretch out your arm to push off his shoulder with your palm.

> The fend-off is only allowed at Under-13 level and above.

ON THE PITCH

Once you have learnt the evasion basics, it is time to develop them further. Even professional rugby players spend many hours sharpening these skills.

BULLDOG

Bulldog is great fun and a good chance to practise tackle avoidance. It is played with four or more players across the width of a rugby pitch.

Bulldog

STEP 1

One player – the bulldog – stands in the middle of the pitch.

STEP 2

The other players have to get across to the other side of the pitch. The bulldog tries to tackle them.

Two bulldogs

STEP 3

Once players are tackled to the ground, they also become bulldogs. Continue until you are all bulldogs.

EVASIVE RUNNING DRILL

You will need 20 cones, 16 players and two balls for this drill. Divide into four groups of four and give each team a name. A team stands in each corner of a 20 metre by 20 metre square. Set out the cones as shown.

1. Teams A and C each have a ball. One player from team A runs through the cones and gives the ball to a player from team B. The B team member then runs through the cones and gives the ball to a member of team A. Repeat this until all players have run. Meanwhile, team C does the same with team D.

2. Next, team A runs diagonally through the cones to give a ball to team D, who return the ball to team A. Team B does the same with team C.

3. Then team A exchanges a ball with team C, and team B with D. You can increase the number of balls per team as the drill goes on.

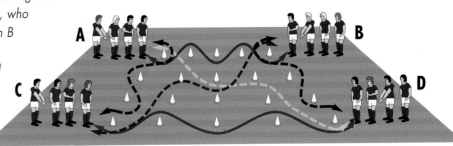

You will need two cones and two players for this drill.

STEP 2

The player runs to the second cone to score a try.

STEP 1

One player runs between two cones. A defender runs to tackle him. The player must sidestep past the defender.

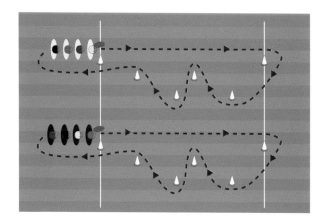

STEP AND SWERVE DRILL

You will need two teams of four or more for this drill.

Divide up your teams. Lay out the cones as shown. The first player in each team sprints up the course with the ball and runs back around the cones. The ball is then passed to the next player in the team. The first team to get all of its players back wins.

STEPPING DRILL

You will need four cones, two balls and two teams of four for this drill.

Place the cones as shown, in a straight line in front of the players. The players run towards the cones, swerve past them and run back to the next in line. The first team to get all of its players back wins.

TOP TIP

Stay on your toes as you approach an opponent – this will make it easier for you to suddenly and unexpectedly change direction.

CATCHING

Being able to catch a rugby ball is a vital skill. Every coach will agree that players cannot work hard enough on their catching and passing.

THE BASIC CATCH

Every rugby player needs to master the basic catch. Buy your own ball and practise throwing and catching, to help you become familiar with it.

STEP 1

Throw the ball in the air. At chest height make a target with your hands. Spread your hands and extend them towards the ball.

STEP 2

Decide at what point to take the ball. Watch it come into your hands.

CATCHING AT A LINE-OUT

Catching at a line-out is a crucial part of a rugby game. It can determine the outcome of a match. Most teams have special jumpers who are lifted by their team-mates to catch a high ball thrown by the hooker.

STEP 1

Wait for the call from the hooker. Crouch down and get ready to leap upwards for the ball. Keep your eye on the ball as you jump into the air. One or two team-mates will lift you as you jump.

STEP 2

Still keeping your eye on the ball, catch it in both hands. Make sure you have it tightly before you call to your lifters to let you down.

STEP 3

As you land, turn your back to the opposing team and throw the ball to your scrum half.

CATCHING A HIGH BALL

Backs often have to catch a high ball, but forwards should also be able to catch one. You can either stand still under a high ball to catch it, or jump for it.

STEP 1

Get under the high ball and keep your eyes on it.

STEP 2

Turn slightly, bringing one shoulder up a bit higher than the other.

STEP 3

Spread your fingers, tuck your elbows in to your body, and reach for the ball.

STEP 4

As the ball comes down into your arms, pull it into your chest.

CATCHING ABOVE THE HEAD

Being able to catch above your head is helpful. It gives you added height if you are challenged for the ball.

STEP 1

When catching, try to 'attack' the ball. Take off on the outside leg and drive your inside knee upwards, towards the ball.

STEP 2

Extend your arms and fingers towards the ball, with your elbows slightly bent.

STEP 3

Watch the ball coming into your hands and bend your elbows on contact. Always try to take the ball at the highest point.

TOP TIP

Make sure your elbows are bent as you catch, as this will help to absorb the impact of the ball.

ON THE PITCH

Catching is all about timing and technique — knowing when to pick the ball from the air and how to hold on to it.

RUGBY TENNIS

This drill is foremost about passing skills, but it is also useful for team communication and awareness.

You will need a ball and two teams of equal size. Position yourselves as shown.

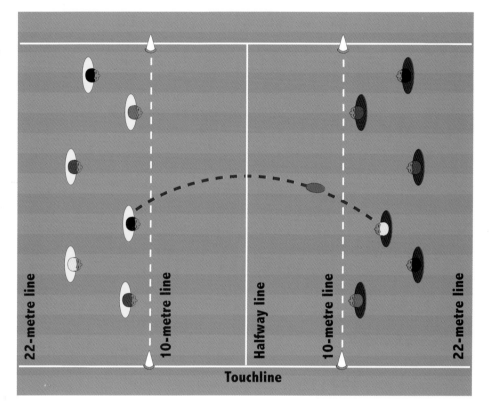

22-metre line   10-metre line   Halfway line   10-metre line   22-metre line

Touchline

STEP 1

Pass the ball over the halfway line at waist height to the other team. If it is not thrown at waist height, the opposing team gets a point.

STEP 2

If the opposing team drops the ball, a point is awarded to the throwing team.

STEP 3

If the ball lands on the ground between players, the opposition gains a point. The team that reaches 15 points first wins.

Learning to jump and catch at the same time is a handy skill. For this drill you will need three players, three cones and one ball.

STEP 1

Place the cones in a straight line five metres apart. One player stands next to each cone.

STEP 2

A player at the end of the line throws the ball to the player at the opposite end. The ball must be thrown only slightly over the raised hands of the player in the middle, so they have a chance of catching it if they jump.

STEP 3

If the middle player catches the ball, the two players swap places. If not, the player at the opposite end of the line catches it and takes a turn at throwing.

THROWING AND CATCHING DRILL

This drill introduces the line-out skill of catching above the head. Four cones and four balls are needed. Place the cones five metres from a central point in a diamond shape.

A catcher stands, arms raised, in the middle of the cones. Four players stand by each of the outer cones. Each one takes a turn trying to hit the catcher's hands. If the ball hits the catcher's hands, he can catch the ball.

TOP TIP

Keep your eye on the ball throughout the catch. If you catch the ball in the air, make sure you have full control before you land.

PASSING

*P*assing is also an essential part of rugby and should be practised often. It will be easier if you stay relaxed while you pass and catch the ball.

BASIC PASS

Even if it seems simple, the basic pass is a vital move to master before moving onto the more complicated passes.

STEP 1

Hold the ball in two hands with your fingers spread across it. Face your chest forward.

STEP 2

Draw the ball back across one hip, keeping your elbows slightly bent. Then sweep the ball towards the target.

STEP 3

Release the ball with a flick of the wrists and fingers.

STEP 4

Follow through with your fingers pointing to the target.

LATERAL PASS

The lateral pass is normally used when the passer is moving. In this drill, positioning your hands at chest height means you will be ready to meet the ball early. For this drill you will need three players and one ball.

STEP 1

Two players stand opposite each other, 10 metres apart. Another player runs between them.

STEP 2

One of the standing players passes the ball to the running player, who catches it.

STEP 3

The runner then swings his arms across his body and passes the ball to the other player.

LINE-OUT THROW

A successful line-out throw is all about getting the ball to the right player. Although the throw is usually taken by the hooker, every person in the team should be able to do it.

STEP 1

Establish a solid foundation. Point your left foot forward and bend your right leg slightly (swap if you are left-handed). Hold the ball with your throwing hand near the back. Bring your arms behind your head, with your elbows fully bent, close to your head.

STEP 2

Shift your weight forward, ready for the throw.

Smooth

STEP 3

Release the ball, using your throwing hand for power and your other hand to guide the ball. Follow your hands through in an arc towards the target and transfer your weight onto your front foot. The path of your hands should be a smooth arc rather than a quick snap.

ON THE PITCH

*W*hether a rugby team is successful or not hinges on good passing. On the pitch, make sure you always pass to a player's hands, not his body.*

QUICK HANDS

Also called 'Fast Hands', this is a favourite with coaches, and great fun for the players. You will need three players and two balls.

STEP 1

All three players stand in a line, several metres apart. The middle player throws a ball in the air above him. The player at the end of the line throws him another ball at the same time.

STEP 2

The middle player catches the ball thrown to him and passes it to the player at the other end of the line before his own ball comes down again.

PASSING DRILL

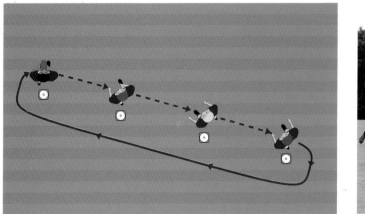

This drill helps with basic passing and catching. You will need four cones, one ball and four players.

Place the cones in a line, 1.5 metres apart. On the whistle, the ball is passed down the line. When the ball reaches the end of the line, the last player runs around to the first cone. Everyone moves down one cone. Repeat until every player has had a turn in each position, and then reverse the direction.

For this passing drill you will need four players, four cones and one ball. Make a square with the four cones, 10 metres by 10 metres.

Scrum half

STEP 1

Each player stands by a cone. One player is the acting scrum half. He throws the ball down the line to the next player, and chases his throw.

STEP 2

Player 2 catches the ball and puts it down on the ground. The scrum half then picks it up, throws it to player 3 and chases it.

STEP 3

The process is repeated with player 4. The scrum half then throws it diagonally and resumes his original position. Player 2 becomes the scrum half. Repeat until every player has had a go at being the scrum half.

Pass... and chase!

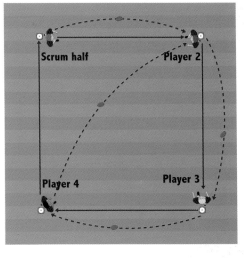

Scrum half   Player 2

Player 4   Player 3

This drill introduces passing skills while on the move. You will need four cones, four players and one ball.

Staggered line

Place the cones in a staggered line, 1.5 metres apart. Each player stands one metre behind a cone. Player 1 walks up to his cone and passes the ball to player 2, who has started to walk up to his cone. Player 2 then passes to Player 3. When player 4 has the ball, he runs around to the first cone and all players move down a cone. Repeat until every player has stood by each cone, and then reverse direction.

TACKLING

A tackle is made with the shoulder, driving into an opponent between the knees and stomach. The power for a tackle comes from the legs, so the longer your feet are on the ground, the stronger your tackle will be.

SIDE TACKLE

The advantage of the side tackle is that you can tackle from either side, while the player is running. Timing is an important factor in bringing your opponent down.

STEP 1

Target your opponent's thighs and lower your body.

STEP 2

Drive with your legs and ready your shoulder for impact.

STEP 3

Grab your opponent round the legs, driving your shoulder into one of his thighs. This should topple your opponent.

STEP 4

Quickly sight the ball. Then, get up on your feet and grab it.

FRONT TACKLE

The front tackle is best attempted by crouching low and driving at your opponent's thighs, as in the side tackle.

STEP 1

Approach your opponent quickly and accelerate into the tackle.

STEP 2

Aim for the area between the knees and stomach, ideally the thighs. Drive in with your shoulder, bend your knees and tackle.

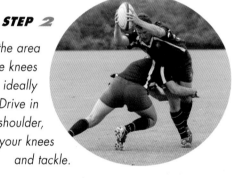

STEP 3

Absorb the impact and twist, so you end up on top of your opponent.

The back tackle is the only way to get hold of an opponent who is running away from you. Timing and determination are essential.

STEP 1

Get as near to your opponent as possible. Target his thighs.

STEP 2

Drive your shoulder into your opponent's thighs. Position your head to one side of his legs.

Always put your head to the 'offside' of the tackle to avoid injury.

STEP 3

Straighten your back and wrap your arms around your opponent's legs.

STEP 4

Land on top of the player and get to your feet quickly.

TOP TIP
Keep low as you tackle. If you tackle high, your opponent will be able to shrug you off easily.

ON THE PITCH

You don't need to be big to carry out a successful tackle. With commitment and the right technique, any player should be able to tackle anyone, regardless of size.

TACKLE BAG DRILL

Using a tackle bag in training is a great way of testing out new tackling skills. For this drill you will need three tackle bags and at least six players.

STEP 1

Three players stand alongside their own tackle bag, holding it up with one hand.

STEP 2

The remaining three players each tackle a bag, knocking it out from underneath the holding player's hand.

STEP 3

The tackler then takes the holding player's place, who joins the tackling queue.

CARRIERS AND TACKLERS

For this drill you will need six players and four cones.

Make a square with the cones, 10 metres by 10 metres. Form two lines on either side of the square – tacklers and ball carriers. On the whistle, the first player in each line runs into the square. The object is for the carriers to score on the tryline, and the tacklers to stop them.

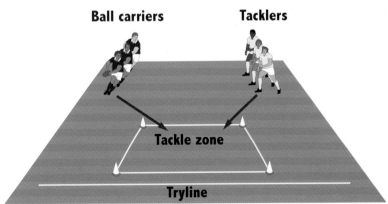

Ball carriers   **Tacklers**

Tackle zone

Tryline

For this drill you will need two or three players, one ball, a tackle bag, and a tryline.

STEP 1

Place the ball on top of a tackle bag. (You might need one player to hold it up.) The second and third players form a line in front of it.

STEP 2

The second player runs and tackles the bag, knocking off the ball.

STEP 3

The third player runs behind, picks up the ball and runs to the tryline to score a try.

For this drill you will need 20 cones, eight or more players, and a tryline.

Set up two staggered lines of cones from the tryline back as shown. Form two lines of players: tacklers and runners. The runners have to run through the cones to the tryline to score. The tacklers have to stop them, after running through their own cones. The tacklers have to dodge more cones than the runners, to give the runners the advantage.

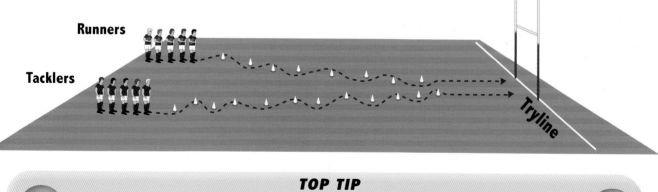

Runners

Tacklers

Tryline

TOP TIP
Wait until you are close to your opponent before performing a back tackle – or you could get a boot in the face!

KICKING

Kicking is not introduced into rugby games until players reach the Under-11 level. It is still an important skill to master early though, so there is no harm practising kicking skills if you are younger.

THE DROP KICK

The drop kick is used to either restart the game, or to kick for a field goal. The ball is dropped and kicked as it bounces back upwards.

STEP 1

Hold the ball in both hands. Sight your target and then look back at the ball. Step forward and raise the ball to your waist.

STEP 2

Drop the ball. At the same time, bring up your knee, ready to kick the ball.

STEP 3

As the ball starts to bounce up, bring your foot through and kick it.

STEP 4

Follow through with your foot. Step up onto the toes of your other foot, using your arms for balance.

THE PUNT

The punt is a valuable skill for every kicker. Usually the fly half, scrum half and fullback take most of the punt kicks, but every player should be able to kick one adequately.

STEP 1

Place your left hand at the front of the ball and right hand at the rear (reverse if you are left-footed). Step forward, planting your non-kicking foot firmly on the ground.

STEP 2

Point the toes of your kicking foot towards the ground. Drop the ball onto it.

STEP 3

Kick the ball as it drops. Follow through with your foot after making contact.

The place kick is used in penalties and conversions. The points at stake can mean the difference between winning or losing a match. Feeling confident and visualising the kick is important when taking the place kick.

STEP 1

Make a mound for the ball with sand or use a cone mount. Tilt the ball so the end is pointing at your target.

STEP 2

Count out some paces from the ball. The number of steps is up to you, but you must stand sideways to the ball, not facing it. Turn your shoulder towards the ball.

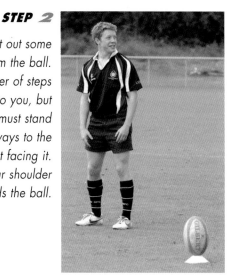

STEP 3

Now run at the ball, getting your non-kicking foot close to it.

STEP 4

Keep your weight over the ball and strike at it. Swing your leg through with the shot.

The grubber kick is a good way of gaining ground with the ball, without running with it. The kick makes the ball unpredictable and hard for the opposition to pick up.

STEP 1

Hold the ball upright. It helps to look where you're kicking it. Keep your eyes on the ball as you drop it.

STEP 2

Kick the upper half of the ball as it falls, leaning over it as you do so.

ON THE PITCH

Once you have kicked the ball, there is only a small chance of regaining it. Always have a good reason to kick. Try to create a smooth rhythm and follow through when you kick.

THE GRUBBER

The grubber kick is best used through gaps between opposition players. Ideally the ball will bounce end over end. For this drill you will need one ball and two cones set up like a football goal.

STEP 1

One player acts as a goalkeeper, inside the goal.

STEP 2

The other player tries to score a goal, as in football.

THE BOMB

The bomb is a high kick that puts the opposing team under pressure. It allows your team-mates time to run up the field and compete for the ball.

STEP 1

Hold the ball vertically and parallel with the body. Sight where you want the ball to go.

STEP 2

Release and kick the ball on its bottom point so it rolls end over end into the air.

THE CHIP KICK

The chip kick can be used to get the ball behind opposition players, as the kicker runs towards them. The kicker or team-mates can then regain the ball. For this drill, you need two teams standing in lines facing one another, 10 metres apart.

STEP 1

The first player from each team runs towards the other – one is carrying the ball. As they get closer, the ball carrier chips the ball over his opponent's head.

STEP 2

The ball carrier catches it on the other side of his opponent.

STEP 3

The ball carrier then hands it to the next person in line. Repeat the drill.

ALL KICKS DRILL

For this drill, split players into pairs with one ball per pair.

One player stands on one line. The other player stands on a line opposite. The two then kick the ball to each other, practising punts, grubbers, high kicks, chips and drop kicks.

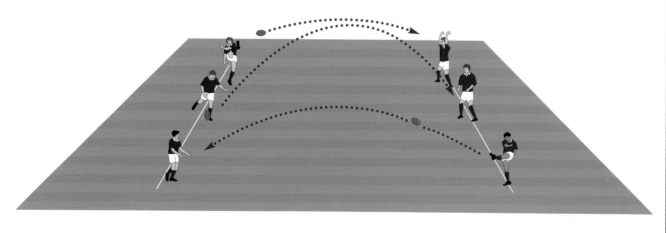

TOP TIP
Before you kick the ball, visualise it going exactly where you want it to go. This will help your accuracy.

THE SCRUM

*T*he number of players that take part in your scrum will depend on your age. In Under-9 teams, scrums have three players per team (and are uncontested – see page 47). In Under-11 teams, there are five players; and in adult scrums, there are eight players.

A scrummage, or scrum for short, takes place as the result of a foul. To form a scrum, the front row players' heads are interlocked with those of the other team. To do this, a player puts his head to the left of his opponent's, with his shoulders higher than their waist. Players must stay linked together for as long as the scrum lasts.

The scrum half from the team that has been awarded possession rolls the ball into the space between the players' feet and those in the scrum compete for possession. Both teams are also trying to push the other team backwards to gain more territory. The hooker then hooks the ball with his foot towards the rear of their scrum. The scrum half collects the ball on the outside of the scrum to restart play.

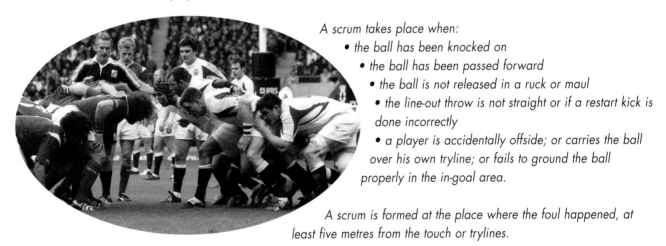

A scrum takes place when:
- *the ball has been knocked on*
  - *the ball has been passed forward*
    - *the ball is not released in a ruck or maul*
      - *the line-out throw is not straight or if a restart kick is done incorrectly*
      - *a player is accidentally offside; or carries the ball over his own tryline; or fails to ground the ball properly in the in-goal area.*

A scrum is formed at the place where the foul happened, at least five metres from the touch or trylines.

If the ball comes straight out of the tunnel, or if it collapses, the scrum is taken again. If the scrum rotates more than 90 degrees the scrum is reformed and awarded to the other side.

1 *Loose head prop*

2 *Hooker*

4 *Second row*

6 *Blindside flanker*

3 *Tight head prop*

9 *Scrum half*

5 *Second row*

7 *Openside flanker*

8 *Number 8*

This drill is great fun to carry out with a team-mate. It will help develop your scrummage skills.

STEP 1

Both players get down on their hands and knees and face each other. They then bind together in the scrum position, as shown.

STEP 2

Then both players push forward into each other, so they come up into a pushing position. Hold the position and then lower back down to the starting position.

This drill will help you develop the skills to bind with a team-mate and push in a scrum. You will need two tackle shields and four players.

STEP 1

Two players stand together holding the shields. The other players lock together with their inside arms around each other's waist.

STEP 2

They then get into a pushing position; the player on the right puts his head between the tackle shields.

STEP 3

The pushers have to try to drive back the players with the tackle shields by half a metre.

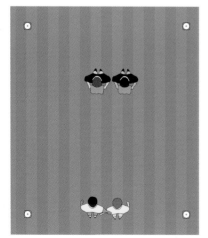

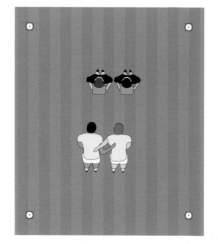

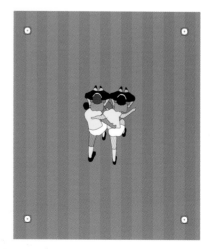

THE RUCK

A ruck is a contest for possession of the ball that occurs when the ball is on the ground and two opposing players meet over it. It occurs when a player has gone to ground and will not release the ball.

To form a ruck, two or more players from each side bind together and compete for the ball by attempting to drive one another from the area. Usually their shoulders are locked.

The players in a ruck cannot pick up the ball, but instead use their feet to 'ruck' the ball backwards to one of their team-mates, who can then put it back into play.

The players in the ruck, or joining the ruck, must have their feet on the ground with their shoulders above waist level, and they must be linked together.

If the ball does not come out of the ruck quickly, the referee will award the forward team the scrum.

This is a good way to develop the pushing skills needed for a ruck. All you need is a wall.

Hold your hands flat against a wall, a little below chest height. Now walk your hands down the wall, stepping backwards but keeping your knees bent. Keep all the weight on your hands. Stop when it becomes uncomfortable, and walk back up.

Three players are needed for this ruck introduction drill.

Players B and C link arms and face A. A pushes into the gap between players B and C and drives them backwards. Player A then breaks through the gap, runs around them and starts again.

> **Remember that you can only join a ruck from behind. If you come in from the side, you'll be penalised.**

A   B C

TOP TIP
When you join a ruck, you should aim to finish several metres past the ball. Concentrate on moving forward, rather than collecting the ball.

THE MAUL

The maul is like a ruck, but the ball is in a player's hands, not on the ground. A maul occurs when the player with the ball is held by one or more opponents and the ball carrier has a team-mate bound to him.

At least three players are needed for a maul: the player with the ball, one team-mate, and one member of the opposition. Once a maul has formed other players may join in, but they must do so on their own side.

The maul ends when the ball goes to ground, or the player with the ball gets free of the maul. If the maul falls apart and the ball does not come out quickly enough, the referee will award the forward-moving side a scrum.

If the ruck stops moving the referee shouts, 'Use it or lose it!' The team in possession has to pass the ball in under five seconds.

This drill will help with the pushing skills needed in a maul. You will need two players and one tackle shield.

One player holds the shield. The other player wraps his arms around the shield and walks his feet backwards until he is in the best position to push with all of his strength. Having found the optimum position, the players swap roles. No actual pushing takes place in this drill.

This drill introduces the skill of getting the ball to the back of the maul.

The players form a line, each one holding onto the player in front. The player at the front hands the ball back to the next player, with one arm. The ball is passed all the way to the back. Then the end player runs to the front and the drill begins again.

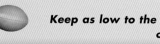
TOP TIP
Keep as low to the ground as possible. If your shoulders and hips are lower than your opponents', you will be in a very strong position.

THE LINE-OUT

A line-out is a way of restarting play when the ball has gone out of the field of play. The line-out takes place at the exact point where the ball crossed the touchline, and is made up of between three and seven players per side. The aim of the line-out is to win the ball and start play.

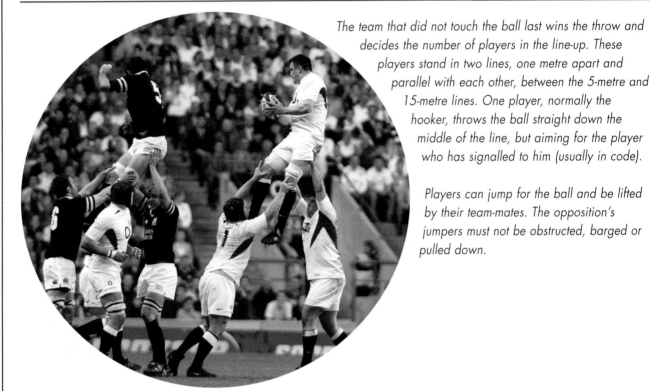

The team that did not touch the ball last wins the throw and decides the number of players in the line-up. These players stand in two lines, one metre apart and parallel with each other, between the 5-metre and 15-metre lines. One player, normally the hooker, throws the ball straight down the middle of the line, but aiming for the player who has signalled to him (usually in code).

Players can jump for the ball and be lifted by their team-mates. The opposition's jumpers must not be obstructed, barged or pulled down.

RULES

These rules must be followed in the line-out.

- *The thrower must not cross into the line of play.*
- *The ball must be thrown straight.*
- *All non-line-out players, except the scrum half, must stand 10 metres back.*
- *No player can use the opposition as support when jumping.*
- *No player can push or hold another player in the line-out.*
- *No player can be lifted before the ball is thrown.*

If these rules are not observed, another line-out or a scrum is awarded to the other team.

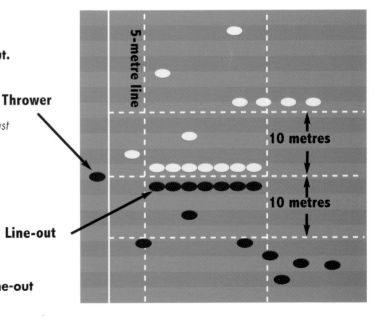

5-metre line

Thrower

Line-out

10 metres

10 metres

LINE-OUT HANDS

This drill enables new players to practise throwing and catching in a line-out.

You will need a ball, four cones and four players. Place the cones in a square with a player standing next to each cone.

Each player throws the ball to the next player in the square. The catchers keep their hands in the air. Continue around the square.

The two most important throwing skills in a line-out are accuracy and timing.

TARGET PRACTICE

This drill helps to develop throwing accuracy.

Pick a target, such as a goalpost. Stand five metres away and throw the ball over your head at the target.

Alternatively, you could use a wooden board fixed to a post as a target.

WARMING UP & STRETCHING

*W**arming up and stretching is an essential part of preparing for any match or training session. This will make you a more agile player and decrease the chances of injury.***

WARMING UP

Before exercise, or even stretching, it is important to warm up your body. Jogging gently for 10 minutes will increase your heart-rate. This gets the blood pumping around your body and prepares your muscles for action. It is also important to warm down after exercise, by repeating the warm-up routine. This will help your body remove waste material (such as lactic acid) from the muscles.

STRETCHING

- Be careful when stretching not to push your body too far.
- Always warm up before stretching.
- Perform each stretch slowly and gently.
- Hold each stretch for 10-15 seconds.
- Never bounce when stretching.
- Make sure you breathe while stretching.
- Push a stretch until you feel it pulling but not hurting.
- Ensure you stretch the muscles you will be using in the match.

LUNGE STRETCH

Lunge forward with your right leg in front, bent at a 90° angle. Your arms should be at waist height.

Repeat with your left leg.

WINDMILLS

Circle both your arms forward. Start with small circles and widen into bigger ones. Repeat for 10 full circles. Then circle your arms backwards. This stretch focuses on the shoulders. Now attempt to circle one arm forwards, while you circle the other arm backwards.

SQUAT

Stand upright with your arms bent in front of you. Hold your hands together as if you were throwing a ball at a line-out. Slowly squat down until your legs are at a 90-degree angle. Rise back up slowly, keeping your back straight. Repeat the squat 10 to 15 times

HIGH SWINGS

Swing your right leg up in front of you to waist height, and back again. Perform six swings then change legs. This stretch focuses on the hamstrings and buttocks. It might help you to hold on to something when you perform this stretch.

HAMSTRING STRETCH

Kneel down and stretch your left leg out in front of you. Pull the toes of your left foot upwards until you feel a pulling sensation along the back of the leg. Hold for 10 seconds and then relax. Repeat the stretch six times and then change legs.

CALF STRETCH

Get on your hands and knees. Raise your knees off the ground. Extend your right leg, keeping balanced on your toes. Gently push your heel down, until you feel it pulling. Repeat six times and then change legs.

DIET

What a rugby player eats is important for success on the field. As well as maintaining a balanced diet, players should also consume fluids before exercising. The food chart below shows how much of each food group you need for a balanced diet.

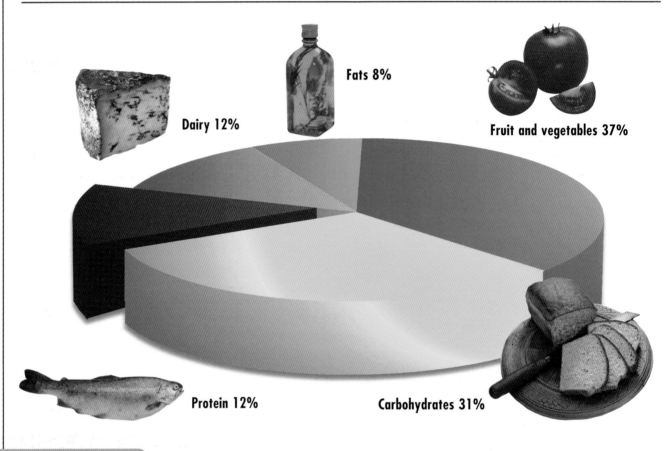

Fats 8%

Dairy 12%

Fruit and vegetables 37%

Protein 12%

Carbohydrates 31%

ENERGY BUSTERS

Training rugby players need lots of carbohydrates to give them enough energy.

Try to avoid sweet and fatty foods, as they lack essential vitamins and minerals.

BEFORE THE MATCH

Eat a high-carbohydrate meal before a match, or any period of exercise, to provide energy.

Eat a light meal the night before a game. On the day, eat a low-fat, high-carbohydrate meal two to three hours before the match starts. A breakfast of toast with jam is ideal. If the game starts later, eat a lunch of pasta with a low-fat sauce. Make sure you are fully hydrated – drink lots of water or sports drinks two to three hours before kick off. This will make up for the water you lose through sweat when playing.

MENTAL ATTITUDE

R ugby is physically demanding, but having the right focus mentally can really make a difference. The mind plays an important role in a player's performance on the pitch. To help you succeed on the day, focus on playing well in the match before it begins. Walking onto the field feeling confident will also help you succeed.

MENTAL PREPARATION

Many professional players have routines that they carry out before a match.

Often these routines involve taking some time before a match to sit quietly and think about the game ahead. During this routine the player should imagine performing well in the game. Think through the different elements of the game and exactly what your role requires. For example, if you are a kicker, imagine converting one try after another. Concentrate on running through the drills you have learnt in training to achieve the winning kick. Imagine the ball sailing over the goalposts. When on the pitch, this image will help you kick a goal more confidently.

MIND AND BODY

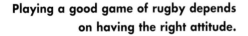

Playing a good game of rugby depends on having the right attitude.

Most coaches agree that attitude determines whether a game is won or lost. Some even say that a good attitude is three times more important than how technically good a player is. A good attitude towards training helps build strength, stamina and all-round fitness. Body and mind have to work together on the pitch. A fit player thinks and reacts more quickly than an unfit player, so is more likely to play well.

It's good to remember that rugby is a sport. Knowing you went onto the field and gave the game your best is more important than winning or losing.

HOW THE FAMOUS DO IT

*T*housands of people around the world play rugby, but only a select few are lucky enough to be paid for it. To reach a professional level, players have to train hard and be extremely determined. The best rugby players spend most of their time exercising, eating properly and getting plenty of rest.

TYPICAL TRAINING DAY – THE ALL BLACKS

7.30-9.00 AM	Breakfast
9.00-9.30 AM	Team meeting
9.30 AM	Depart to training
10.00 AM-12.00 PM	Training
12.30-1.30 PM	Recovery and lunch
2.00 PM	Team-naming press conference
3.00-5.00 PM	Weights and rehab
6.00 PM	Sponsor presentation
7.00 PM	Dinner

TYPICAL MATCH DAY – THE ALL BLACKS

12.30 PM	Lunch
2.30 PM	Walkthrough
3.30 PM	Pre-game meal
5.00 PM	Advance staff to stadium
6.00 PM	Team meeting and depart to stadium
7.35 PM	Kick off
10.00 PM	Post-match sponsor functions
11.00 PM	Post-match meal

TRAVELLING TO MATCHES

Many international teams from around the world travel long distances to play rugby in different countries.

Even teams from small regional clubs are expected to travel to nearby towns and cities to play. Teams tend to travel at least one day before the match, so they are in good time to prepare for it. In general, rugby players can expect to spend many hours travelling, whether it be driving up the road by coach, or flying to another continent.

Top international players make a lot of money playing rugby.

Household names like Jonny Wilkinson can afford to retire at a young age. The most famous players often benefit from sponsorship deals and ongoing advertising work. But the earnings of most rugby players are far lower then football players, and often club players are paid very little.

International rugby players are very famous. What they do and say is often reported in the press.

Important players are always expected to give a post-match television interview, even if their team has lost the game. There are hundreds of magazines, websites, TV programmes and radio shows all dedicated to rugby. As well as giving their opinions on the game, rugby players usually support their communities, by coaching junior teams or speaking at local clubs.

RULES

There are many rules in rugby and there are different rules for different age groups. The general rules are listed below, along with the age at which they apply. The referee ensures both teams play by the rules, which are there to make the game fair for everybody.

OBJECTIVE

To score more points than the other team. Players achieve this by scoring tries, conversions, drop goals and penalties in the opposite team's goal area. A coin is tossed to determine which team kicks off. The ball is set down and must be kicked at least 10 metres into the opposition's half; otherwise the opposition have the choice of whether to take a scrum or a throw-in on the halfway line. A drop kick from the halfway line will restart the game after a penalty or drop goal has been scored. The team that did not score kicks.

TIME

A game of rugby lasts for two halves of 40 minutes, with a 10-minute interval in between. Teams swap ends after the interval. Any injury time is added on at the end of each half.

POINTS

A try is scored when a player puts the ball on the ground with 'downward pressure' inside the opposition's in-goal area between the tryline and dead-ball line. A try is worth five points. The ball can then be converted, which means it is placed and kicked over the goalposts for two points. A drop kick over the goalposts (a drop goal) is worth three points, and can be played at any point during the match.

RUCK

A ruck is a contest for possession of the ball that occurs when the ball is on the ground and two or more opposing players meet over it and bind together. No player in a ruck can pick up the ball. See pages 34-35.

MAUL

A maul occurs when a ball carrier is held by a member of the opposite team and a member from his own team binds to him. A maul can only be joined from behind, not the sides. See pages 36-37.

KNOCK ON

In rugby the ball can never be passed forwards – all passes must be made backwards. So, if the ball is accidentally knocked forward at any point, a scrum will be awarded to the other team.

SCRUMMAGE

A scrummage, or 'scrum', takes place as a result of an infringement of the rules. To form a scrum, front row players bind together and interlock their heads with those of the other team. See pages 32-33.

LINE-OUT

A line-out is awarded when the ball crosses the touchline. A line of players from each team stand opposite each other, and compete for the ball when it is thrown between them. See pages 38–39.

TACKLING

Tackling means grabbing the player in possession of the ball, holding on to them or pulling them down to the ground. A tackled player on the ground must release the ball and cannot rejoin play until he is standing. Players can only be tackled when they have the ball. If a player is tackled without the ball, a penalty is awarded to the opposition.

MARK

A player may call for the mark when he catches a high ball inside his own 22-metre line or in-goal area. As he catches the ball, he shouts 'Mark!' and the referee will award the player a free kick.

OFFSIDE

A player is offside if he is in front of a team-mate who has the ball, or during a ruck or scrum if he wanders in front of the offside line. Only the number 8 can leave a scrum to collect the ball.

YELLOW AND RED CARDS

The yellow card represents a caution, shown to a player who has acted in an unsporting way or who has committed a serious foul. The player then leaves the field to sit in the sin bin – a bench outside the pitch – for 10 minutes. The red card means a player is immediately excluded from the rest of the game. A red card is shown for violent or dangerous behaviour.

PENALTY

A penalty is awarded when a team has committed a foul. The penalty kick is taken by the opposing team and is kicked like a conversion. It is worth three points. The ball can be also be kicked into touch.

RULES FOR DIFFERENT AGE GROUPS

Under 9s:

Full-contact tackling, rucks and mauls are allowed. Three-man scrums are also allowed but they are uncontested, so the team who puts the ball into the scrum must win it and there is no pushing. There is no kicking at this age group. Games have nine players per side and are 30 minutes long.

Under 10s:

From this age, contested scrums and contested two-man line-outs are allowed – but still no kicking.

Under 11s and Under 12s:

Scrums are now five players, with two rows. The games are 12 per side. Line-outs can contain four players and tactical kicking is introduced in a limited form. The laws of the game follow nearly all those of the senior game. There are also kick-offs, conversions and free-kicks. The games increase from 30 minutes to 40 minutes.

Under 13s to Under 17s:

At the Under-13 level, the games become 15-a-side full-contact games and the fend-off is now permitted. The playing time gradually increases from 25 minutes to 35 minutes each way. There are slight rule variations from the adult games. These can be found on www.rfu.com/regulations.

GLOSSARY

BREAKDOWN *The period immediately after a tackle and the ensuing ruck. During this time teams compete for possession of the ball, initially with their hands and then using their feet in the ruck.*

DROP KICK *A kick for goal in which the ball is dropped and kicked as it bounces.*

DROP-OUT *A way of restarting the game, usually after the ball has gone over the defending team's dead-ball line. A drop-out is taken from either the 5-metre, 15-metre or 22-metre line, depending on the age group.*

EVASION *Dodging to avoid being tackled.*

FEED *Putting the ball into the scrum.*

GRUBBER KICK *A kick where the ball bounces along the ground.*

KICK FOR TOUCH *To kick the ball directly out of bounds.*

KNOCK ON *When the ball is accidentally knocked forward by a player. A penalty is given to the other team.*

LATERAL PASS *A pass to the side.*

OFFSIDE *Being in front of a team-mate with the ball when your team is the attacking team, or when a player is out of position during a ruck or scrum.*

PENALTY KICK *Method to restart play after a major foul has occurred. The team awarded the penalty can kick a field goal, kick into touch or opt for a scrum.*

PITCH *The playing field.*

RED CARD *This is shown for violent or unsporting behaviour, and means the player is immediately sent off.*

SIN BIN *A bench off the playing field where players sit after being shown a yellow card.*

TACKLE *When the ball carrier is wrestled to the ground by an opponent.*

TOUCH *Out of bounds.*

TRY *A score by touching the ball down, with pressure and under control, in the opposition goal area. Tries are worth five points.*

YELLOW CARD *A yellow card is awarded for repeated infractions to the rules. A player who is shown a yellow card is sent to the 'sin bin' for 10 minutes.*

LISTINGS

Rugby Football Union
*Rugby House, Rugby Road
Twickenham, Middlesex TW1 1DZ
Tel: +44 (0)870 405 2000
www.rfu.com*

International Rugby Board
*Huguenot House, 35-38 St Stephen's Green
Dublin 2, Ireland
Tel: +353 1 240 9200
www.irb.com*

Australian Rugby Union
*Ground Floor, 29-57 Christie Street
St Leonards NSW 2065, Australia
Tel: +61 2 8005 5555
www.rugby.com.au*

South African Rugby Football Union
*PO Box 99, Newlands 7725, South Africa
www.sarugby.co.za*